United States Government Accountability Office

Report to Congressional Committees

I0448129

June 2013

BUILDING PARTNER CAPACITY

Actions Needed to Strengthen DOD Efforts to Assess the Performance of the Regional Centers for Security Studies

Highlights of GAO-13-606, a report to congressional committees

BUILDING PARTNER CAPACITY

Actions Needed to Strengthen DOD Efforts to Assess the Performance of the Regional Centers for Security Studies

Why GAO Did This Study

DOD has emphasized innovative and low-cost approaches to build the defense capacity of foreign partners, and it uses its five Regional Centers to administer programs to foster partnerships and deepen foreign officials' understanding of U.S. objectives. The conference report accompanying the fiscal year 2013 National Defense Authorization Act (H.R. Conf. Rep. No. 112-705) mandated GAO to conduct a study of the Regional Centers. GAO's report (1) describes how the Regional Centers' activities compare with those of other DOD training and education organizations, and (2) evaluates the extent to which DOD has developed and implemented an approach to oversee and assess the Regional Centers' progress in achieving DOD priorities. This report also provides information on the process used to approve Regional Center requests to waive reimbursement of the costs for nongovernmental and international organizations that participate in the Regional Centers' activities. GAO reviewed public law and departmental directives and conducted an analysis comparing aspects of the Regional Centers with other selected DOD training and education institutions.

What GAO Recommends

GAO recommends that DOD develop measurable goals linked to key programming priorities for the Regional Centers, metrics for assessing performance against these goals, and a methodology to assess the Regional Centers' progress in achieving DOD priorities. DOD generally agreed with the recommendations.

View GAO-13-606. For more information, contact Sharon Pickup at (202) 512-9619 or pickups@gao.gov or Charles Michael Johnson, Jr. at (202) 512-7331 or johnsoncm@gao.gov.

What GAO Found

The Department of Defense's (DOD) five Regional Centers for Security Studies (Regional Centers) share similarities and differences with other DOD institutions that provide training and education, including professional military education, advanced degree-conferring, and professional development institutions, in terms of curriculum topics, targeted audience, and program format. GAO found that they all offer training and educational programs and activities to help participants understand security and military matters and to enhance their knowledge, skills, and experiences in these matters. However, there are notable differences in that the Regional Centers generally focus on helping foreign participants understand and respond to regional security issues; generally target a foreign civilian and military personnel audience; and offer shorter and typically less formal courses of study. The Regional Centers support DOD policy objectives with curricula designed to enhance security and foster partnerships through education and exchanges. By contrast, other DOD training and education organizations focus their curricula on military operations and leadership. While the Regional Centers' target audience is foreign civilian and military officials, the other DOD educational organizations typically aim their programs and activities at U.S. servicemembers at all career levels. Regional Center participants generally do not earn credit toward a degree, and the offered courses, conferences, and workshops are of shorter duration ranging from days to weeks. DOD's professional military education and advanced degree-conferring institutions are accredited and generally offer longer, more formal courses that provide participants the opportunity to earn advanced degrees.

DOD has taken some steps to enhance its oversight of the Regional Centers' plans and activities, but its ability to determine whether the Regional Centers are achieving departmental priorities remains limited because it has not developed an approach for assessing progress. DOD has defined roles and responsibilities, issued relevant guidance that reflects departmental objectives, and established a governance body and planning process to facilitate information sharing and to achieve more integrated decision making. However, DOD has not developed an approach that includes measurable goals and objectives, metrics for assessing performance, or a methodology to assess the Regional Centers' progress in achieving DOD priorities, to include clarifying how it will use performance data provided by the Regional Centers. GAO's prior work has found that achieving results in government requires a comprehensive oversight framework that includes clear goals, measurable objectives, and metrics for assessing progress, consistent with the framework established in the Government Performance and Results Act. The Regional Centers report various types of performance data, such as summaries of past activities. While DOD has established a governance body to assist in monitoring the Regional Centers' plans and activities, the body has not identified how it will use performance information to assess the Regional Centers' progress toward achieving department priorities. Conducting routine assessments using measurable goals and objectives, with metrics to evaluate progress, and a methodology for using performance information to include defining the role of the governance body would provide DOD a sounder basis for assessing the Regional Centers' progress in achieving results, and for better determining the allocation of resources.

_____ United States Government Accountability Office

Contents

Figures

Abbreviations

DOD	Department of Defense
DSCA	Defense Security Cooperation Agency
GPRA	Government Performance and Results Act
NGO/IO	Nongovernmental and International Organization
OUSD Policy	Office of the Under Secretary of Defense for Policy
Regional Centers	Regional Centers for Security Studies
State	Department of State

GAO

U.S. GOVERNMENT ACCOUNTABILITY OFFICE

441 G St. N.W.
Washington, DC 20548

June 28, 2013

The Honorable Carl Levin
Chairman
The Honorable James M. Inhofe
Ranking Member
Committee on Armed Services
United States Senate

The Honorable Howard P. "Buck" McKeon
Chairman
The Honorable Adam Smith
Ranking Member
Committee on Armed Services
House of Representatives

In recent years, the Department of Defense (DOD) has emphasized security cooperation approaches to build the defense capacity of foreign partners and advance the U.S. objective of international peace and cooperation. For example, strategic guidance issued by the Secretary of Defense in January 2012 highlighted the importance of enhancing the defense capacity of foreign partners in order to share the costs and responsibilities of global leadership.[1] Termed "building partner capacity," this approach, according to DOD officials, represents the way to reduced long-term U.S. presence while protecting the territory of other nations. The strategic guidance stated that a fiscally constrained environment will require innovative, low-cost, and small-footprint activities toward building partner capacity. These activities include training, educating, and assisting foreign countries' civilian and military personnel in becoming more proficient at defense-related decision making, providing security to their populations, and protecting their resources and territories.

As part of the department's efforts to build partner capacity, DOD relies on its Regional Centers for Security Studies (Regional Centers) to coordinate with the geographic combatant commands in developing training and educational programs around the globe to enhance security,

---

[1]Department of Defense, *Sustaining U.S. Global leadership: Priorities for 21st Century Defense* (Washington, D.C.: Jan. 5, 2012).

GAO-13-606 Building Partner Capacity

deepen foreign officials' understanding of the United States, and foster bilateral and multilateral partnerships. In addition to the Regional Centers, DOD and the Department of State (State) offer other programs and activities to provide training and education to foreign military and civilian personnel. These include, among other programs and activities, officer exchange programs, educational opportunities at U.S. professional military schools, and programs designed to assist foreign nations with building more effective defense institutions. In fiscal year 2012, the Regional Centers obligated approximately $101.4 million. Subject to certain requirements, the Regional Centers are permitted to use a portion of these funds to waive the reimbursement of the costs for foreign officials and other personnel, such as representatives of nongovernmental and international organizations, to participate in the Regional Centers' programs and activities.

In our prior work we have identified challenges that DOD faces in managing its initiatives to build the defense capacity of foreign partners, as well as key practices that could provide opportunities for DOD to more effectively manage these efforts. Specifically, we have found instances in which DOD had not consistently defined measures to evaluate progress, and in which reporting on the progress and effectiveness of some defense capacity-building activities had been limited. For example, in 2012 we reported that because the National Guard's State Partnership Program did not have agreed-upon goals or metrics, DOD could not assess progress toward achieving program goals.[2] Our work has emphasized how, among other things, setting clear goals can help stakeholders understand what defense capacity-building programs seek to accomplish, and how establishing mechanisms to evaluate progress can help ensure that programs have long-term impact.[3] A list of our related work that identifies challenges DOD has faced in its efforts to build the defense capacity of partners can be found at the end of the report.

The conference report accompanying the National Defense Authorization Act for Fiscal Year 2013 (Pub. L. No. 112-239) mandated us to conduct a

---

[2]GAO, *State Partnership Program: Improved Oversight, Guidance, and Training Needed for National Guard's Efforts with Foreign Partners*, GAO-12-548 (Washington, D.C.: May 15, 2012).

[3]GAO, *Building Partner Capacity: Key Practices to Effectively Manage Department of Defense Efforts to Promote Security Cooperation*, GAO-13-335T (Washington, D.C.: Feb. 14, 2013).

GAO-13-606 Building Partner Capacity

study of DOD's Regional Centers.[4] In this report, we (1) describe how the Regional Centers' activities compare with those of other DOD training and education organizations, and (2) evaluate the extent to which DOD has developed and implemented an approach to oversee and assess the Regional Centers' progress in achieving DOD priorities. In addition, we are providing information about the process used by DOD and State for approving and monitoring Regional Center requests to waive reimbursement of the costs for nongovernmental and international organizations that participate in the Regional Centers' activities.

To address these objectives, we interviewed officials from the Office of the Under Secretary of Defense for Policy (OUSD Policy), the Defense Security Cooperation Agency (DSCA), and each of the five Regional Centers: the Africa Center for Strategic Studies, the Asia-Pacific Center for Security Studies, the William J. Perry Center for Hemispheric Defense Studies, the George C. Marshall European Center for Security Studies, and the Near East South Asia Center for Strategic Studies. We also interviewed officials from the six geographic combatant commands and State's Bureau of Political-Military Affairs. To determine how the Regional Centers' activities compare with those of other DOD training and educational programs and activities, we identified three areas to use in comparing program features—curriculum topics, target audience, and program format. We reviewed the Joint DOD-State Foreign Military Training Report,[5] the Interagency Working Group International Exchanges and Training Report,[6] and other DOD documents, and we identified 17 DOD organizations that implement programs identified in these documents for our analysis, and compared characteristics of these organizations' programs and activities with those of the Regional Centers. The results of our analysis are not generalizable to DOD training and education programs and activities outside of those included in the scope of our work.

To determine the extent to which DOD has developed and implemented an approach to oversee the Regional Centers' progress and assess their

---

[4]H.R. Conf. Rep. No. 112-705, at 838-839 (2012).

[5]Department of Defense and Department of State, *Foreign Military Training, Fiscal Years 2010 and 2011, Joint Report to Congress* (Washington, D.C.: n.d.).

[6]*Interagency Working Group on U.S. Government-Sponsored International Exchanges and Training, Fiscal Year 2011 Annual Report* (Washington, D.C.: n.d.).

progress in achieving DOD priorities we examined DOD guidance[7] as well as DOD annual reports, Regional Center program and budget plans, and other documentation, and we referred to the Government Performance and Results Act (GPRA) as amended by the GPRA Modernization Act of 2010[8] and our prior work that identifies elements that constitute a comprehensive oversight framework.[9] We also interviewed officials from OUSD Policy, from DSCA, and from the Regional Centers to obtain their perspectives on the processes used to oversee the Regional Centers' programs and activities and to assess their performance in achieving DOD priorities.

To identify the process used by DOD and State to approve and monitor Regional Center requests to waive reimbursement of costs for nongovernmental and international organizations that participate in the Regional Centers' activities, we reviewed DSCA guidance identifying the procedures for submitting requests and the criteria applied to consideration of waivers for nongovernmental and international organizations. We discussed the process with DSCA and State officials and obtained information on the waivers requested, as well as the amounts waived, between fiscal years 2009 and 2012.

We conducted this performance audit from August 2012 to June 2013 in accordance with generally accepted government auditing standards. Those standards require that we plan and perform the audit to obtain sufficient, appropriate evidence to provide a reasonable basis for our findings and conclusions based on our audit objectives. We believe that the evidence obtained provides a reasonable basis for our findings and conclusions based on our audit objectives. A more detailed description of our scope and methodology is included in appendix I.

---

[7]Department of Defense Directive 5200.41, *DOD Centers for Regional Security Studies*, (July 30, 2004, certified current as of Dec. 5, 2008).

[8]Pub. L. No. 103-62 (1993); Pub. L. No. 111-352 (2011).

[9]See, for example, GAO-12-548 and *Preventing Sexual Harassment: DOD Needs Greater Leadership Commitment and an Oversight Framework*, GAO-11-809 (Washington, D.C.: Sept. 21, 2011).

Background

DOD's Emphasis on Initiatives to Build the Defense Capacity of Partner Nations

According to the 2010 Quadrennial Defense Review Report, a component of DOD's strategy to prevent and deter conflict is to help build the capacity of partners to maintain and promote stability, and such an approach requires working closely with U.S. allies and partner nations to leverage existing alliances and create conditions to advance common interests. Such "building partner capacity initiatives" comprise a broad range of security cooperation and security assistance activities.

Security cooperation is the broad term used by DOD for those activities taken to build relationships that promote specified U.S. interests, build partner nation capabilities for self-defense and coalition operations, and provide U.S. forces with access both in peacetime and during contingencies. These activities are carried out under various statutory authorities. For example, DOD may conduct activities with partner nations, such as sending out military liaison teams, exchanging military personnel between units, or conducting seminars and conferences in theaters of operations under Title 10 U.S. Code.[10] DOD also conducts security cooperation activities through security assistance programs authorized by Title 22 U.S. Code.[11] These Title 22 programs are a part of U.S. efforts to provide foreign assistance through military assistance and sales.

DOD Regional Centers' Mission

The five Regional Centers for Security Studies (Regional Centers) support DOD's objective to build the defense capacity of partner nations. The Regional Centers' activities include education, exchanges, research, and information sharing. The Regional Centers conduct in-residence courses, in-country seminars, and conferences, among other activities, that address global and regional security challenges such as terrorism and maritime security. DOD policy states that a core Regional Center mission is to assist military and civilian leaders in the region in developing strong defense establishments and strengthening civil-military relations in

---

[10]See, for example, 10 U.S.C. §168.

[11]See, for example, 22 U.S.C. §§ 2311–2322 (Foreign Military Assistance) and 22 U.S.C. §§ 2347–2347h (International Military Education and Training).

GAO-13-606 Building Partner Capacity

a democratic society.[12] In doing so, the Regional Centers are expected to coordinate with the department's geographic combatant commands in developing and implementing activities for their region. Table 1 lists the five Regional Centers, the year in which each was established, their locations, and their corresponding geographic combatant commands.

Table 1: Overview of DOD's Regional Centers for Security Studies

Regional Center	Year established	Location	Primary geographic combatant command
George C. Marshall European Center for Security Studies	1993	Garmisch-Partenkirchen, Germany	U.S. European Command
Asia-Pacific Center for Security Studies	1995	Honolulu, Hawaii	U.S. Pacific Command
William J. Perry Center for Hemispheric Defense Studies	1997	Washington, D.C.	U.S. Southern Command U.S. Northern Command
Africa Center for Strategic Studies	1999	Washington, D.C.	U.S. Africa Command
Near East South Asia Center for Strategic Studies	2000	Washington, D.C.	U.S. Central Command

Source: DOD.

Note: While each Regional Center supports a primary geographic combatant command, the Regional Centers also conduct programs and activities to support other geographic combatant commands.

Figure 1 depicts each Regional Center's primary geographic area of focus, which are generally consistent with each center's corresponding geographic combatant command's area of responsibility.

---

[12]Department of Defense Directive 5200.41.

Figure 1: The Regional Centers' Primary Geographic Areas of Focus

Africa Center for Strategic Studies

Asia-Pacific Center for Security Studies

William J. Perry Center for Hemispheric Defense Studies

George C. Marshall European Center for Security Studies

Near East South Asia Center for Strategic Studies

Source: GAO analysis of DOD documents

In fiscal year 2012, the Regional Centers obligated approximately $101.4 million. Appendix II provides an overview of each Regional Center including a description of fiscal year 2012 resources. Subject to certain requirements, the Regional Centers are permitted to use a portion of these funds to waive the reimbursement of the costs for foreign officials and other personnel, such as representatives of nongovernmental and international organizations, to participate in the Regional Centers' programs and activities. Appendix III provides a more detailed discussion of DOD's process to waive the reimbursement costs for personnel representing nongovernmental and international organizations.

Regional Centers' Programs and Activities Share Some Similarities with Those Offered by Other DOD Organizations, but There Are Notable Differences

DOD provides training and education opportunities to U.S. and foreign participants by means of various institutions, among which are the five Regional Centers; professional military education and degree-conferring institutions; and professional development institutions. For our review, we analyzed training and educational programs and activities administered by 17 selected DOD institutions, and compared them with those administered by the Regional Centers for the following three attributes: curriculum topics, targeted audience, and program format. (See appendix I for a full list of institutions in our review.) The main similarities and differences we observed in comparing them are described below.

DOD Organizations Administer Various Types of Training and Educational Programs and Activities

DOD provides U.S. and foreign participants with a variety of training and educational programs and activities through its five Regional Centers, its professional military education and advanced degree-conferring institutions, and its professional development institutions. For example, the Regional Centers, in accordance with DOD Directive 5200.41, support departmental policy objectives with activities designed to enhance security, foster partnerships, improve national security decision making, and strengthen civil-military relationships through education, exchanges, research, and information sharing.[13] Professional military education and advanced degree-conferring institutions aim to develop U.S. military personnel (enlisted and officer) with expertise and knowledge appropriate to their grade, branch, and military professional specialty. Examples of professional military education and advanced degree-conferring institutions include the National Defense University and the Naval Postgraduate School, respectively. DOD also administers training and

---

[13]Department of Defense Directive 5200.41.

educational programs and activities to U.S. and foreign participants through various professional development institutions for the purpose of providing developmental opportunities and enhancing their mission-related knowledge, skills, and experience. Examples of DOD's professional development institutions include the Defense Acquisition University and the Center for Civil-Military Relations.

Regional Centers' Programs and Activities Share Similarities and Differences with Those Offered by Other DOD Institutions

Programs and activities administered by the Regional Centers and other DOD professional military education and advanced degree-conferring institutions as well as professional development institutions have similar features in that they all

- offer curriculum topics intended to help participants enhance knowledge and skills on security and military matters;
- target members of the military; and
- feature program formats that include in-residence courses; seminars, conferences, workshops; distance learning; and in-country instruction.

However, some differences exist among the Regional Centers and the other programs administered by DOD organizations. Specifically:

- Regional Centers focus on bringing participants together for courses intended to foster understanding of regional security challenges and to strengthen the professional skills needed to develop effective strategies. In contrast, professional military education institutions generally focus on military operations and leadership; and advanced degree-conferring institutions and professional development institutions generally focus on professional knowledge, skills, and experiences.
- The Regional Centers' audience is generally civilian and military officials from other countries. In contrast, professional military education institutions and advanced degree-conferring institutions target U.S. military officials.
- The Regional Centers' program format is generally shorter than an academic year, and its completion does not count toward an academic degree. In contrast, professional military education institutions and advanced degree-conferring institutions offer degree and certificate programs that can take over a year to complete.

Table 2 summarizes a comparison of programs and activities administered by DOD's Regional Centers, professional military education and advanced degree-conferring institutions, and professional development institutions, in terms of curriculum topics, targeted audience, and program format. The checkmarks in the table indicate that we found the attribute is generally descriptive of the category, as we found exceptions to the attribute in some cases.

Table 2: Comparison of DOD Programs and Activities by Curriculum Topic, Target Audience, and Program Format

Attribute	Regional Centers	Professional military education institutions[a]	Advanced degree-conferring institutions[b]	Professional development institutions[c]
Curriculum topics				
Convening U.S. and other country participants to understand regional security challenges and to develop cooperative strategies	✓			
Military operations and leadership in support of the U.S. national security strategy		✓		
Knowledge, skills, and experience related to security professions			✓	✓
Target audience				
U.S. civilian				✓
U.S. military		✓	✓	✓
Foreign civilian	✓			✓
Foreign military	✓			✓
Program format				
Accredited degree program		✓	✓	
In-residence courses	✓	✓	✓	✓
Seminars, conferences, and workshops	✓	✓	✓	✓
Distance learning	✓	✓	✓	✓
In-country training and education	✓	✓	✓	✓

Legend: ✓ = The attribute descr bed is applicable to one or more institutions in the category.

Source: GAO analysis of DOD documents.

[a]The professional military education institutions included in our review are: the Air University, Army Command and General Staff College, Army JFK Special Warfare School, Army War College, Joint Special Operations University, Marine Corps War College, National Defense University, Naval War College, and Western Hemisphere Institute for Security Cooperation.

[b]The advanced degree-conferring institutions included in our review are: the Air Force Institute of Technology and Naval Postgraduate School.

[c]The professional development institutions included in our review are: the Center for Civil Military Relations, Defense Acquisition University, Defense Institute of International Legal Studies, Defense Institute for Medical Operations, Defense Resource Management Institute, and NATO School.

To further elaborate on the information in table 2, the following paragraphs describe similarities and differences for each of the attributes we reviewed.

GAO-13-606 Building Partner Capacity

Curriculum Topics

We found that the Regional Centers, professional military education and advanced degree-conferring institutions, and professional development institutions are similar in that they all offer programs and activities to help a participant understand security and military matters and to enhance his or her knowledge and skills.

The Regional Centers focus their programs and activities on addressing OUSD Policy and geographic combatant command priorities and bringing participants together to understand regional security challenges and to develop cooperative strategies to address them. For example, the Asia-Pacific Center for Security Studies administers a Comprehensive Security Responses to Terrorism course designed to broaden knowledge and improve skills in assessing terrorism threats in the Asia-Pacific region and to develop a community of professionals to collaborate on regional and global issues. Another example is the Africa Center's *African Executive Dialogue*, which brings together African and U.S. senior officials to discuss how African countries can work together and with external stakeholders on Africa's key security challenges. A further example is the Marshall Center's Seminar on Trans-Atlantic Civil Security, which is designed to improve the homeland defense capacity and skills, across the whole of government, needed to prevent and respond to natural or man-made disasters or terrorist attacks.

Moreover, each of the Regional Centers devotes significant programmatic effort to establishing, developing, and sustaining alumni networks. For example, officials at the Asia-Pacific Center told us that they track the progress of and provide support for the establishment of alumni chapters in Asia-Pacific countries, as well as helping to coordinate alumni events sponsored by these chapters. According to its program plan for fiscal year 2013, the Near East South Asia Center plans to conduct 10 alumni events in the region to promote continual engagement with and among participants who have attended the center's core programs and promote collaboration on current regional security issues.

In contrast, professional military education institutions' programs and activities focus on instructing U.S. servicemembers in military operations and leadership in support of the U.S. national security strategy. For example, the National Defense University administers a Combating Terrorism Strategies and Policies course in which students examine the ongoing challenge to U.S. national security posed by the threat of international terrorism and the ways in which the United States is attempting to prevent future terror attacks. The advanced degree-conferring institutions focus on instructing U.S. military professionals on security-related knowledge and skills, such as operations research, logistics, and information system management. For example, the Naval Postgraduate School administers an Applied Mathematics Course in which students learn advanced mathematical techniques applicable to game theory and network design. The professional development institutions address professional security-related knowledge, skills, and experiences, such as consequence management, law enforcement, and decision making. For example, the Defense Acquisition University administers a variety of training courses that members of the defense acquisition workforce can use toward certification in various acquisition fields, such as systems acquisition, cost analysis, and contracting. In another example, the Defense Institute for Medical Operations administers an Emergency Management Strategies for Senior Leaders course to review and exercise executive-level principles for emergency management, disaster planning, and corrective action plan implementation.

Target Audience

In terms of target audience, we found that the Regional Centers, professional military education and advanced degree-conferring institutions, and professional development institutions are similar in that all of them include institutions that target programs and activities to members of the military.

We found that the Regional Centers are distinct in that participants in their programs and activities are generally from other countries, either civilians or members of the military. In 2012, 82 percent of the participants at the five Regional Centers were civilians or members of the military from other countries. According to officials and participants with whom we spoke, the preponderance of foreign participants provide U.S. participants with the unique experience of being in the minority during the discussion of U.S. security policy decisions and their impacts around the world. Further, officials stated that the Regional Centers intentionally invite executive-level civilian officials as well as representatives from nongovernmental organizations, international organizations, and the private sector to ensure a broad, whole-of-government audience. Past participants of the Africa Center for Strategic Studies have included six current and former heads of state.

By contrast, professional military education and advanced degree-conferring institutions are primarily attended by members of the U.S. military at all career levels. For example, about 85 percent of the students enrolled in 2012 at the Air University were U.S. servicemembers, while foreign military students made up less than 2 percent of the student body.

Similarly, U.S. servicemembers comprise the majority of the student population at other DOD professional military education institutions. One notable exception is the Western Hemisphere Institute for Security Cooperation, which provides professional military education to Latin American military officers and noncommissioned officers.

Program Format

In terms of program format, the Regional Centers, professional military education and advanced degree-conferring institutions, and professional development institutions all offer programs and activities in the form of in-residence courses; seminars, conferences, and workshops; distance learning; and in-country instruction.

The key distinctions between the Regional Centers and the other organizations in program format is that professional military education and advanced degree-conferring institutions offer degrees and certificates programs that are accredited by an independent accrediting institution.[14] Professional military education or advanced degree-conferring programs generally entail completion of academic courses of instruction over a longer period for which a participant can earn credit toward a degree or certificate. For example, participants at the Army Command and General Staff College can earn a Master of Military Art and Science degree. Further, the Army Command and General Staff College and the three other services' Command and General Staff Colleges are accredited institutions. In another example, Naval Postgraduate School certificate, Master's, and Ph.D. programs can take up to 4 years to complete.

In contrast, Regional Centers and some professional development institutions' programs and activities are generally not creditable toward an academic degree and are generally shorter than an academic year, ranging from a few days to a few weeks. For example, a William J. Perry Center for Hemispheric Defense Studies course on homeland security entails a 3-week online phase, a 3-week in-residence phase, and a 3-week paper-writing phase.

---

[14]The goal of accreditation is to ensure that education provided by institutions of higher education meets acceptable levels of quality. Accrediting agencies, which are private educational associations of regional or national scope, develop evaluation criteria and conduct peer evaluations to assess whether or not those criteria are met. Institutions and programs that request an agency's evaluation and that meet an agency's criteria are then "accredited" by that agency.

Although the Regional Centers generally offer shorter-duration courses on a range of security topics, some centers provide participants with opportunities to obtain credit for their attendance. For example, the George C. Marshall European Center for Security Studies offers two programs that can earn participants credit toward advanced degrees. U.S. and foreign officers completing coursework at the center can earn credit toward a Master's in International Security Studies from the Bundeswehr University in Munich, Germany, and the center also administers a Senior Service Fellows program whereby U.S. servicemembers can earn credit toward graduate degrees at their respective service's war college. In addition, although the Perry Center for Hemispheric Defense Studies does not award degrees, some Latin American institutions of higher learning, such as the Universidad Francisco Marroquin, located in Guatemala City, Guatemala, award credit for successful completion of the center's courses.

The professional development institutions also generally offer shorter-duration courses. For example, the majority of Defense Institute for Medical Operations courses are 4 to 7 days in length, and Defense Institute of International Legal Studies courses range from 1 to 4 weeks.

DOD Has Taken Steps to Enhance Oversight of the Regional Centers Plans and Activities but Its Ability to Assess Their Progress Remains Limited

DOD has taken some steps to enhance its oversight of the Regional Centers' plans and activities, but it does not have a sound basis to evaluate their progress in achieving DOD priorities because it has not developed an assessment approach that includes measurable goals and objectives with metrics or established a methodology for using the performance information it collects. Our prior work[15] has found that achieving results in government requires a comprehensive oversight framework that includes clear goals, measurable objectives, and metrics for assessing progress, consistent with the framework established in the Government Performance and Results Act.[16]

DOD Has Taken Steps to Enhance Oversight of Regional Centers' Plans and Activities

Since 2005, DOD has taken several specific steps to enhance oversight of the Regional Centers, including defining roles and responsibilities, issuing guidance, and establishing a governance body and planning process. Specifically:

- *Roles and Responsibilities*: OUSD Policy, according to DOD Directive 5200.41, is responsible for providing policy guidance and oversight and conducting reviews of the effectiveness of the Regional Centers in achieving DOD objectives, including resource allocation, management practices, and measures of effectiveness.[17] In 2005, DOD designated the DSCA director as the executive agent for the Regional Centers and assigned it the responsibility for programming, budgeting, and management of the resources necessary to support their operation and providing them with needed staffing.[18]
- *Guidance*: OUSD Policy issues guidance to the Regional Centers that assigns priorities to them reflecting national security and departmental

---

[15]See, for example, GAO-12-548, GAO-11-809, and *Military Personnel: DOD Needs an Oversight Framework and Standards to Improve Management of Its Casualty Assistance Programs,* GAO-06-1010 (Washington, D.C.: Sept. 22, 2006).

[16]The Government Performance and Results Act of 1993, Pub. L. No. 103-62 (1993) was recently amended by the Government Performance and Results Modernization Act of 2010, Pub. L No. 111-352, 124 Stat. 3866 (2011).

[17]Department of Defense Directive 5200.41.

[18]Deputy Secretary of Defense, DTM-05-002, *Executive Agent for DOD Regional Centers for Security Studies* (Washington, D.C.: Sept. 29, 2005).

GAO-13-606 Building Partner Capacity

objectives. For example, in January 2013, OUSD Policy issued fiscal year 2013 guidance incorporating policy priorities identified in DOD's January 2012 Defense Strategic Guidance,[19] and instructing the Regional Centers to address those priorities as they plan and execute programs.[20] DSCA issues planning guidance that requires the Regional Centers to develop program plans to meet the OUSD Policy priorities within their projected funding baseline and existing authorities.[21] The fiscal year 2014-2015 guidance states that each Regional Center's program plan, among others requirements, should include a cover letter signed by the Regional Center director or program manager, background and concept papers for core program and significant events, a completed 2-year budget submission, and a list of efficiency initiatives to be implemented. Further, DOD Directive 5200.41 states that the Regional Centers are required to develop and implement their activities according to guidance from the geographic combatant commanders.[22]

- *Governance body and planning process*: In December 2011, DOD established a governance body within OUSD Policy, called the Principal Deputy Assistant Secretary of Defense Board,[23] that provides guidance for and monitoring of the Regional Centers' activities and plans. According to DOD officials, OUSD Policy established the board intending to facilitate coordination and information sharing among different OUSD Policy offices, and to achieve more integrated decision making on policies, plans, programs, and budgets. DOD officials told us that before the board's establishment, each Regional Center reported to its respective OUSD Policy stakeholders, and the opportunity for broader information

---

[19]Department of Defense, *Sustaining U.S. Global Leadership.*

[20]Office of the Under Secretary of Defense (Policy), *FY 13-14 Priorities for the Regional Center for Security Studies* (Washington, D.C.: Jan. 23, 2013).

[21]Defense Security Cooperation Agency, *Fiscal Year 2014-2015 Program Planning Guidance* (Arlington, VA.: January 2013).

[22]We found that four of the geographic combatant commands provide general objectives or tasks for the Regional Centers to support their programs and activities, and two commands issue guidance that identifies specific programs and tasks to be implemented by their respective Regional Centers.

[23]The board is chaired by the OUSD Policy Chief of Staff, and its members include the OUSD Policy regional and functional Principal Deputy Assistant Secretaries of Defense, the Director of DSCA, and the Deputy Under Secretary of Defense for Strategy, Plans, and Forces.

sharing was minimal. The board's activities include, in 2011, establishing a 16-month planning process to guide how the board and OUSD Policy stakeholders will provide guidance and oversee the development of plans and activities of the Regional Centers. As shown in figure 2, key steps in the planning cycle include

- identifying priorities and providing guidance to the Regional Centers;
- providing a means with which the Regional Center directors can update stakeholders on prior-year activities and future-year plans;
- coordinating proposed Regional Center program plans with OUSD Policy offices, the geographic combatant commands, and the board; and
- reviewing Regional Centers' budgets and program plans.

Figure 2: Overview and Timeline of OUSD Policy's 16-month Planning Process for the Regional Centers for Security Studies (Regional Centers) (Initiated in 2011)

May
- Office of the Under Secretary of Defense for Policy (OUSD Policy) begins coordination of priorities and guidance

August
- Principal Deputy Assistant Secretary of Defense (PDASD) Board meets and issues updated guidance and priorities

October
- Regional Centers brief prior year results and outcomes and receive guidance from OUSD Policy offices at Regional Center Roundtable

January
- Defense Security Cooperation Agency (DSCA) issues fiscal guidance and criteria for program plan submission

February-March
- Regional Centers finalize and coordinate program plan with geographic combatant commands and OUSD Policy offices

March-April
- Regional Centers brief program plans to OUSD Policy offices

April
- Regional Centers Director's brief program plans to PDASD board

May
- Regional Centers submit program plans to DSCA

June-September
- Regional Centers submit required budget documents to DSCA

October
- Regional Centers execute program plan

Source: GAO analysis of DOD documents.

We found that OUSD Policy largely follows the above planning process and has implemented the steps it describes; however, some steps, such as the issuance of the Regional Center priority guidance, were sometimes delayed.

DOD Has Not Yet Developed an Approach with Key Elements Needed to Assess the Regional Centers Progress in Achieving DOD Priorities

Notwithstanding DOD's efforts to enhance its oversight of the Regional Centers plans and activities described above, we found that OUSD Policy is limited in its ability to review the effectiveness of the Regional Centers in achieving DOD objectives because it has not yet developed an assessment approach that includes key elements, such as identifying measurable goals and objectives linked with performance metrics that would provide a means by which to evaluate their progress in achieving departmental priorities, or established a methodology for how it would use the performance information it collects to assess that progress. Our prior work[24] has found that achieving results in government requires a comprehensive oversight framework that includes clear goals, measurable objectives, and metrics for assessing progress, consistent with the framework established in the Government Performance and Results Act.[25]

DOD Has Not Developed an Assessment Approach That Includes Measureable Goals and Objectives

DOD has not developed an assessment approach that includes measurable goals and objectives for the Regional Centers for use in assessing their progress towards meeting DOD's priorities. In February 2011 and again in January 2013, OUSD Policy identified strategic goals and a number of priority objectives for the Regional Centers.[26] However, many of the strategic goals were broad and not measurable, such as the goal to facilitate engagement with foreign participants to promote critical thinking on global security challenges. Additionally, although OUSD Policy identified priority objectives specific to each Regional Center in the January 2013 guidance, we found the priority objectives were still not measurable in many cases. For example, the priority objectives listed in

---

[24]See, for example, GAO-12-548, GAO-11-809, and GAO-06-1010.

[25]The Government Performance and Results Act of 1993, Pub. L. No. 103-62 (1993) was recently amended by the Government Performance and Results Modernization Act of 2010, Pub. L No. 111-352, 124 Stat. 3866 (2011).

[26]Under Secretary of Defense (Policy), *Policy Guidance for the Department of Defense Regional Centers* (Washington, D.C.: Feb. 28, 2011); *FY 13-14 Priorities for the Regional Center for Security Studies.*

the guidance for all of the Regional Centers include "contributing to an increased emphasis on security cooperation and building partnership capacity efforts in the Asia-Pacific and Middle East," and ensuring that the United States is a security partner of choice for other nations. Additionally, the guidance documents list broad priority objectives for each Regional Center, such as supporting national security strategy development for one Regional Center, and addressing the growing threat of transnational organized crimes and illicit trafficking for another Regional Center.

DOD Has Not Established Metrics to Assess Progress

According to DOD Directive 5200.41, OUSD Policy is responsible for conducting reviews of the effectiveness of the Regional Centers in achieving DOD objectives.[27] However, DOD has not established performance metrics or other indicators to assess the Regional Centers' progress in achieving DOD priorities. We have previously reported that performance metrics that measure progress are necessary for management oversight.[28] OUSD Policy officials acknowledge difficulties in developing metrics to assess security cooperation programs, such as those administered by the Regional Centers, observing that it is inherently challenging to link a security cooperation activity with desired effects. These officials described past and current efforts intended to provide information that could be used to help develop metrics. For example:

- In 2010, OUSD Policy tasked the Regional Centers with developing a comprehensive set of measures of effectiveness by which progress toward objectives could be assessed. In November 2010 the Regional Centers submitted a plan.
- Thereafter, OUSD Policy contracted with the RAND Corporation to review the November 2010 plan.[29] In September 2011, RAND concluded that the measures of effectiveness identified in the plan had some weaknesses.[30] RAND recommended that the Regional Centers develop a more comprehensive set of metrics and proposed a framework for developing them.

---

[27]Department of Defense Directive, 5200.41.

[28]GAO-12-548.

[29]Regional Centers for Security Studies, *Regional Center Enterprise: Measures of Effectiveness* (November 2010).

[30]The RAND Corporation, National Defense Research Institute, *Review of the Regional Center Enterprise Measures of Effectiveness Plan*, (Santa Monica, CA: September 2011).

- On the basis of the results, the Principal Deputy Assistant Secretary of Defense Board concluded that further study was needed. Therefore, in July 2012, OUSD Policy contracted with RAND to conduct a study to evaluate the effect of the Regional Centers and to determine their contribution toward fulfilling OUSD Policy strategy objectives. DOD expects RAND to publish a final report in September 2013. According to OUSD Policy officials, they believe the RAND study will provide additional insights into the metrics or indicators that could be used to evaluate the Regional Centers' performance.

We recognize and have previously reported that it is difficult to establish performance measures for outcomes that are not readily observable and that in some cases systematic, in-depth program evaluation studies may be needed in addition to performance measures.[31] Such program evaluation studies are conducted periodically and include context in order to examine the extent to which a program is meeting its objectives.[32] Further, our prior work has shown that performance measures should focus on core activities that would help managers assess whether they are achieving organizational goals.[33]

DOD Has Not Established a Methodology for Assessing Progress

OUSD Policy has not established a methodology for assessing the Regional Centers' progress in achieving DOD priorities, to include clarifying how it will use performance data provided by the Regional Centers and clearly identifying the role of its governance board in the assessment process. We found that, individually, the Regional Centers collect data on their programs and activities, and while their efforts vary, they all generally capture output and anecdotal data, such as summaries of activities, events, attendee demographics, and participant days, as well as the results of program surveys they conduct. For example:

- One Regional Center summarized its assessment efforts as conducting after-action reports, class evaluations, before and after program surveys, and trip reports.

---

[31]GAO-12-548; and *Performance Measurement and Evaluation: Definitions and Relationships,* GAO-11-646SP (Washington, D.C.: May 2011).

[32]GAO-12-548 and GAO-11-646SP.

[33]GAO, *Defense Business Transformation: Improvements Made but Additional Steps Needed to Strengthen Strategic Planning and Assess Progress,* GAO-13-267 (Washington, D.C.: Feb. 12, 2013).

- One Regional Center sends surveys to the attendees' supervisors to collect data on the attendee's work performance and, if applicable, any improvement in job performance subsequent to their attendance at Regional Center programs, as well as to elicit the supervisors' perspectives on the utility of the courses and its applicability to their careers. Additionally, the center has developed an internal, searchable database to store useful data and outcomes collected from surveys, e-mails, and personal anecdotes.
- Two Regional Center use a crosswalk that identifies how its programs and activities support stakeholder priorities, as well as the effects of its activities.

The Regional Centers provide data to OUSD Policy and DSCA on both their expected achievements and their past activities. For example, as required by DOD, the Regional Centers include in their program plans expected achievements of their specific programs and a discussion of how they expect their programs will support OUSD Policy priorities.[34] Additionally, as discussed earlier in this report, the Regional Center directors brief the Principal Deputy Assistant Secretary of Defense Board on their past activities. In our review of the board presentations in January 2013, we found that the board members had the opportunity to ask questions as well as request additional information on specific aspects of their activities.

However, OUSD Policy has not established a methodology or clarified how it will use this performance information to assess the Regional Centers' performance against expected outcomes or in achieving DOD priorities. Furthermore, although DOD established a governance body to assist in monitoring the Regional Center's plans and activities, DOD officials acknowledge that the role of the governance body in assessing the Regional Centers' performance is not clearly defined. For example, the governance body has not identified how it will consider the performance information provided by the Regional Centers in making decisions or demonstrated how the newly established planning process will integrate the performance information to assess the Regional Centers' progress towards OUSD Policy strategic goals and priority objectives.

---

[34]Defense Security Cooperation Agency, *Fiscal Year 2013-2014 Program Planning Guidance*.

Conducting routine assessments using measurable goals and objectives with metrics to evaluate progress would provide DOD with a sounder basis for determining whether the Regional Centers are achieving results, as well as for allocating resources. Until measurable program goals and objectives linked with performance metrics are implemented, DOD cannot fully assess or adequately oversee the Regional Centers. Moreover, with clearly defined roles and responsibilities for assessing the Regional Centers, oversight mechanisms such as the governance body could prove beneficial in evaluating the Regional Centers' performance in achieving DOD priorities, as well as the performance of other DOD initiatives to build partner nations' capacity.

Conclusions

Effective management of efforts to build the defense capacity of foreign partners will help DOD steward its resources to achieve its strategic priorities and will likely better position the U.S. government to respond to changing conditions and future uncertainties around the world. As a component of DOD's broader effort, the Regional Centers provide an opportunity for the U.S. government to strengthen cooperation with foreign countries. While DOD has expressed challenges entailed in establishing metrics to capture the effects of a program premised on relationship-building and has taken steps to study the matter, it has yet to establish an initial set of metrics. We note the importance for DOD to have measurable goals and objectives linked with performance metrics, which would form the foundation for an oversight framework. While DOD has taken positive steps by establishing a new governance body and updating DOD guidance applying to the Regional Centers for fiscal year 2013, DOD does not yet have a process to assess the Regional Centers' progress. Conducting routine assessments using measurable goals and objectives, with metrics to evaluate progress, and a methodology for using performance information to include defining the role of the governance board, would provide DOD a sounder basis for assessing the Regional Centers' progress in achieving results and better determining the allocation of resources. Moreover, DOD's ability to assess the Regional Centers' performance would provide Congress with the information it needs as it evaluates current and similar programs and considers future funding levels.

Recommendations for Executive Action

To enhance DOD's ability to determine whether the Regional Centers are achieving departmental priorities, we recommend that the Secretary of Defense direct the Under Secretary of Defense for Policy to

- develop an approach to assess the Regional Centers' progress in achieving DOD priorities, including identifying measurable goals and objectives, metrics, or other indicators of performance, and
- develop a methodology for using performance information, to include defining the role of the governance board in the process.

Agency Comments and Our Evaluation

We provided a draft of this report to DOD and State for comment. DOD provided written comments which are reprinted in appendix IV. In its written comments, DOD partially concurred with our first recommendation and concurred with our second recommendation. DOD also provided technical comments, which we have incorporated into the report, as appropriate. State did not provide any comments on the draft.

DOD partially concurred with our first recommendation that the Secretary of Defense direct the Under Secretary of Defense for Policy to develop an approach to assess the Regional Centers' progress in achieving DOD priorities, including identifying measurable goals and objectives, metrics, and other indicators of performance. In its comments, DOD noted that our recommendation should take into account that a process already exists for Regional Center program development and approval, which requires the Regional Centers to identify specific program goals that meet policy objectives. DOD further noted that the department recognized the need to improve the identification of measurable goals and objectives, metrics, or other indicators of performance, and is already taking steps to address this issue. DOD suggested that we revise our recommendation to state that DOD should bolster the current approach to assess the Regional Centers' progress in achieving DOD priorities, including identifying measurable goals and objectives, metrics, and other indicators of performance that appropriately measure the essential aspects of the Regional Centers' mission.

As noted in our report, we recognize that DOD has a process for developing and reviewing Regional Center programs and that the department has established policy priorities for the Regional Centers. The report also notes that the Regional Centers include in their program plans expected achievements of their specific programs and a discussion of how they expect their programs will support OUSD Policy priorities. However, we note that DOD's January 2013 guidance to the Regional Centers contained priority objectives that were not measurable in many cases. Further, our report describes past and current DOD efforts that could be useful toward identifying metrics to assess Regional Center progress in achieving DOD priorities. However, DOD has not yet established an initial set of metrics. Without those key elements, we do not believe that DOD has a sound approach to assess the Regional Centers' progress. Therefore we believe our recommendation is stated appropriately.

We are sending copies of this report to the appropriate congressional committees. We are also sending copies to the Secretary of Defense; the Under Secretary of Defense for Policy; and the Secretary of State. In addition, the report will also be available on our website at http://www.gao.gov.

If you or your staff have questions about this report, please contact Sharon L. Pickup at (202) 512-9619 or pickups@gao.gov, or Charles Michael Johnson, Jr. at (202) 512-7331. Contact points for our Offices of Congressional Relations and Public Affairs may be found on the last page of this report. GAO staff who made key contributors to this report are listed in appendix V.

Sharon L. Pickup
Director
Defense Capabilities and Management

Charles Michael Johnson, Jr.
Director
International Affairs and Trade

Appendix I: Scope and Methodology

To assess how the Regional Centers for Security Studies' (Regional Centers) programs and activities compared with those of other DOD organizations that provide training and educational programs and activities, we completed the following steps. First, we researched U.S. government programs, activities, and initiatives providing training and education to foreign civilian and military individuals. We reviewed two U.S. government reports that provided comprehensive information on training and education provided to foreign civilian and military professionals: the Interagency Working Group on U.S. Government-Sponsored International Exchanges and Training fiscal year 2011 Annual Report; and the Foreign Military Training Fiscal Years 2010 and 2011 Joint Report to Congress. The Interagency Working Group Annual Reports provide a review of activities over a given fiscal year and they include the previous fiscal year's inventory of programs detailing the scope of federal international exchanges and training. The Foreign Military Training Report is jointly completed by DOD and the Department of State (State) and provides information on all military training provided to foreign military personnel by DOD and State during the previous fiscal year and all such training proposed for the current fiscal year. In addition, we reviewed the Defense Institute of Security Assistance Management's *The Management of Security Cooperation* (Green Book); the Defense Security Cooperation Agency's fiscal year 2013 Budget Request; and Army Regulation 12-15, *Joint Security Cooperation Education and Training*. The Defense Institute of Security Assistance Management Green Book is the publication employed by the institute for instruction covering the full range of security cooperation and security assistance activities. The Defense Security Cooperation Agency's fiscal year 2013 Budget Request identifies specific security cooperation activities administered by the agency. The Joint Security Cooperation Education and Training regulation prescribes policies, procedures, and responsibilities for training international personnel. By reviewing these documents, we identified a comprehensive inventory of U.S. security cooperation and security assistance programs that provide training and education to foreign nationals. Second, we excluded programs that: (1) did not have national security and policy as their primary focus, or (2) taught specific skill- or tactical-level training, such as language or flight training. We then compared these programs against the legislation establishing the Regional Centers and the DOD directive governing their activities. On the basis of this comparison, we focused our selection on the subset of training and education programs and building partner capacity initiatives that, like the Regional Centers, support DOD priorities by enhancing security, fostering partnerships, and assisting regional leaders to develop strong defense establishments. We learned that the programs identified in these first two steps of our selection process could be classified in two categories: (1) DOD institutions that provide training and education and (2) DOD and State programs and authorities that provide funds for U.S. citizens and foreign nationals to attend these institutions. Because one of the Regional Centers' activities is to provide for education and exchanges by conducting in-residence courses, in-country seminars, and conferences, among other activities, we focused our next selection step on identifying training and educational program providers. Third, we completed additional research on DOD institutions that provide training and education. We conducted a preliminary review of each institution by reading a description of it, and we again excluded those that provide tactical-level training on skills not addressed by the Regional Centers. The team collected additional information about these institutions by completing online research, reviewing documentation collected during the engagement, and requesting data and information from each institution. On the basis of this research and review, we identified and selected 17 organizations for this analysis; the organizations are DOD institutions that provide training and education, but U.S. citizens and foreign nationals that attend these institutions are, in some instances, funded by DOD and State programs and authorities. Where applicable, we also analyzed the various schools under each institution.

1. Air Force Institute of Technology (part of Air University)
2. Air University
3. Army Command and General Staff College
4. Army JFK Special Warfare School
5. Army War College
6. Center for Civil Military Relations
7. Defense Acquisition University
8. Defense Institute for Medical Operations
9. Defense Institute of International Legal Studies
10. Defense Resource Management Institute
11. Joint Special Operations University
12. Marine Corps War College
13. National Defense University
14. NATO School

15. Naval Postgraduate School

16. Naval War College

17. Western Hemisphere Institute for Security Cooperation

Fourth, we identified which attributes to examine. For this engagement, we selected three similar areas for comparison—curriculum topics, target audience, and program type and format. In prior work, GAO has compared programs by examining various program attributes, such as the populations targeted, the types of services provided, or the program's geographic focus. As the analysis entailed comparing the Regional Centers to the above 17 selected training and educational providers, we concluded a review should examine the curriculum offered by each provider and that the populations targeted and program format attributes were applicable. We determined that these attributes we selected were appropriate for comparing training and educational providers because they explain the curriculum focus of each organization's primary training and educational efforts, who they engage in these efforts, and their method of engagement. The results of our analysis are not generalizable to DOD training and education programs and activities outside of those included in the scope of our work.

To determine the extent to which DOD has developed and implemented an approach to oversee the Regional Centers and assess their progress in achieving DOD priorities, we evaluated relevant documentation and interviewed knowledgeable officials. Specifically, we reviewed the legislation establishing the Regional Centers, DOD guidance[1] governing their activities, and the 2010 and 2011 DOD annual reports to Congress on Regional Center activities; the Office of the Under Secretary of Defense (OUSD) Policy fiscal year 2011-2012 and 2013-2014 policy guidance and DSCA Fiscal Year 2014-2015 program planning guidance to the Regional Centers, and the Regional Centers' program plans submitted in response; and briefing documents concerning the establishment of the Principal Deputy Assistant Secretary of Defense Board. In January 2013 we attended and observed the fourth meeting of this board. We also reviewed a prior study conducted by the RAND Corporation, contracted by OUSD Policy, to evaluate the Regional

---

[1]Department of Defense Directive 5200.41, *DOD Centers for Regional Security Studies,* (July 30, 2004, certified current as of Dec. 5, 2008).

Centers' measures-of-effectiveness plan, and met with RAND officials. In completing site visits to the Regional Centers, we reviewed documentation relating to their missions, anticipated outcomes, scheduled and proposed activities, program development processes, and outreach to alumni. We also observed classes and conferences in progress and met with international attendees. Additionally, to identify oversight mechanisms for the Regional Centers, we reviewed key geographic combatant command documents to include guidance issued to Regional Centers and theater planning documents, and we interviewed key command officials. We also referred to our prior work that identifies elements that constitute a comprehensive oversight framework, and to prior work that identifies the relationship between performance management and program evaluation.[2]

To provide information about the process used by DOD and State to approve and monitor Regional Center requests to waive reimbursement of costs for nongovernmental and international organizations that participate in the Regional Centers' activities, we reviewed relevant legislation and DSCA guidance identifying the procedures for submitting requests and the criteria applied to consideration of waivers for nongovernmental and international organizations. We discussed the process with DSCA and State officials and obtained information on the various waivers requested, as well as the amounts waived, between fiscal years 2009 and 2012.

To address all of our objectives, we collected information by interviewing or communicating with officials in

(1) the Office of Under Secretary of Defense for Policy (OUSD Policy), specifically the following subordinate offices:
   a) Principal Deputy Assistant Secretary of Defense for Partnership Strategy and Stability Operations,
   b) Principal Deputy Assistant Secretary of Defense for International Security Affairs,

---

[2]See, for example, GAO, *State Partnership Program: Improved Oversight, Guidance, and Training Needed for National Guard's Efforts with Foreign Partners*, GAO-12-548 (Washington, D.C.: May 15, 2012); *Preventing Sexual Harassment: DOD Needs Greater Leadership Commitment and an Oversight Framework*, GAO-11-809 (Washington, D.C.: Sept. 21, 2011); and *Performance Measurement and Evaluation: Definitions and Relationships*, GAO-11-646SP (Washington, D.C.: May 2011).

GAO-13-606 Building Partner Capacity

    c)   Deputy Assistant Secretary of Defense African Affairs,

    d)   Principal Deputy Assistant Secretary of Defense for Russia, Ukraine & Eurasia,

    e)   Principal Deputy Assistant Secretary of Defense for Western Hemispheres Affairs,

    f)   Principal Deputy Assistant Secretary for Defense—Asia Pacific Security Affairs,

    g)   Deputy Assistant Secretary of Defense for Strategy, and

    h)   Principal Deputy Assistant Secretary of Defense for Special Operations & Low-Intensity Conflict;

(2)   the Defense Security Cooperation Agency;

(3)   each of the five Regional Centers:

    a)   the Africa Center for Strategic Studies,

    b)   the Asia-Pacific Center for Security Studies,

    c)   the George C. Marshall European Center for Security Studies,

    d)   the Near East South Asia Center for Strategic Studies, and

    e)   the William J. Perry Center for Hemispheric Defense Studies;

(4)   each of the six geographic combatant commands:

    a)   U.S. Africa Command,

    b)   U.S. Central Command,

    c)   U.S. European Command,

    d)   U.S. Northern Command,

    e)   U.S. Pacific Command, and

    f)   U.S. Southern Command;

(5)   the Global Center for Security Cooperation;

(6)   the following State bureaus:

    a)   Bureau of African Affairs,

    b)   Bureau of East Asian and Pacific Affairs,

    c)   Bureau of Political-Military Affairs, and

    d)   Bureau of Western Hemisphere Affairs;

(7)   the U.S. Agency for International Development; and

(8)   the RAND Corporation.

We conducted this performance audit from August 2012 through June 2013 in accordance with generally accepted government auditing standards. Those standards require that we plan and perform the audit to obtain sufficient, appropriate evidence to provide a reasonable basis for our findings and conclusions based on our audit objectives. We believe that the evidence obtained provides a reasonable basis for our findings and conclusions based on our audit objectives.

About the Center

Location: Washington, D.C.

Satellite locations: Addis Ababa, Ethiopia, and Dakar, Senegal

Founded: 1998

Mission: The Africa Center for Strategic Studies supports U.S. foreign and security policies by strengthening the strategic capacity of African states to identify and resolve security challenges in ways that promote civil-military cooperation, respect democratic values, and safeguard human rights.

Priorities:
- Counter violent extremism and counterterrorism
- Peacekeeping and stability
- Promote and perserve partnerships
- Security-sector transformation
- Transnational security challenges

Courses:
- Next Generation of African Security Leaders
- Senior Leaders Seminar
- African Executive Dialogue
- Managing Security Resources in Africa
- African Defense Attaché Seminar
- Introduction to African Security Issues
- Topical Outreach Program Series
- Countering Violent Extremism and Radicalization
- Leadership and Accountability in Countering Illicit Trafficking
- Maritime Safety and Security
- Security Sector Transformation

Alumni: 5,193 (as of September 2012)

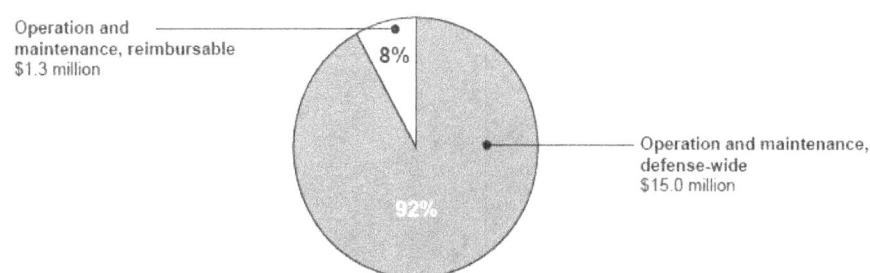

Fiscal Year 2012 Funding

Operation and maintenance, reimbursable $1.3 million — 8%

Operation and maintenance, defense-wide $15.0 million — 92%

Total funding: $16.3 million

Source: GAO analysis of DOD documents.

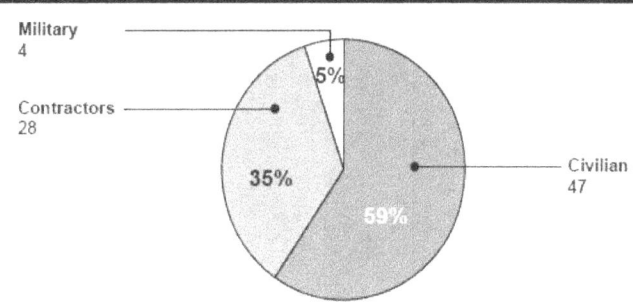

Fiscal Year 2012 Personnel

Military 4 — 5%

Contractors 28 — 35%

Civilian 47 — 59%

Total personnel: 79 (as of September 2012)

Source: GAO analysis of DOD documents.

Note: Total may not add due to rounding.

Area of Focus

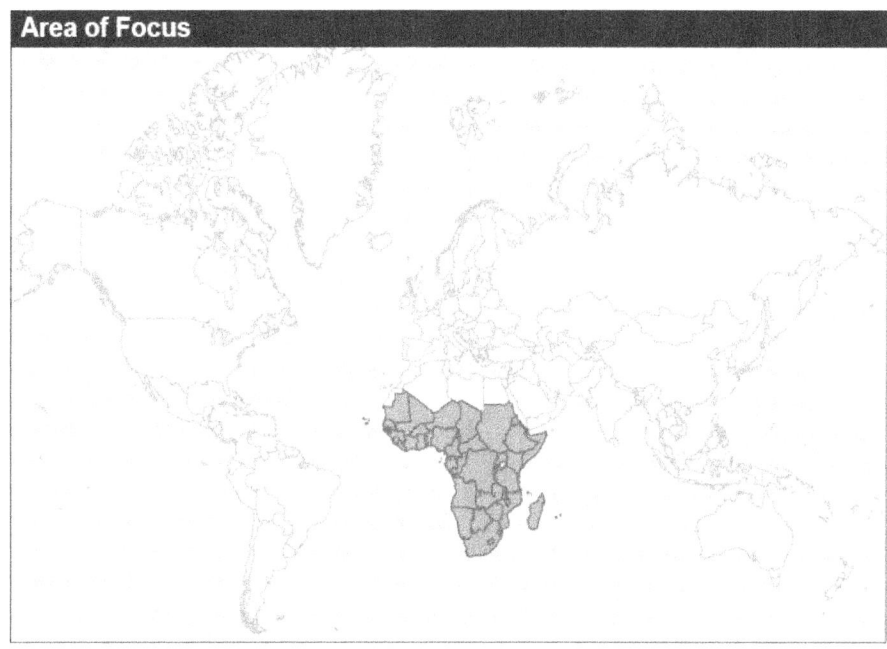

Source: GAO analysis of DOD documents.

Asia Pacific Center for Security Studies

About the Center

Location: Honolulu, Hawaii

Founded: 1995

Mission: Building capacities and communities of interest by educating, connecting, and empowering security practitioners to advance Asia-Pacific security.

Priorities: Contribute to regional stability by focusing on:
- Counterterrorism
- Defense institution building
- Humanitarian assistance and disaster response
- Maritime and border security
- Promotion of multilateral cooperation /confidence-building
- Space policy and cyber-security
- Stability and peacekeeping
- Transnational security threats

Courses:
- Advanced Security Cooperation Course
- Comprehensive Crisis Management Course
- Comprehensive Security Responses to Terrorism Course
- Transnational Security Cooperation Senior Executive Course

Alumni: 7,068 (as of January 2013)

Fiscal Year 2012 DOD Operation and Maintenance Funding

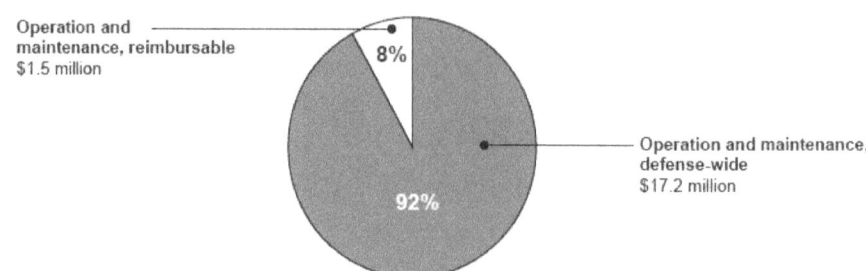

Operation and maintenance, reimbursable $1.5 million — 8%

Operation and maintenance, defense-wide $17.2 million — 92%

Total funding: $18.8 million

Source: GAO analysis of DOD documents.

Note: Total may not add due to rounding.

Fiscal Year 2012 Personnel

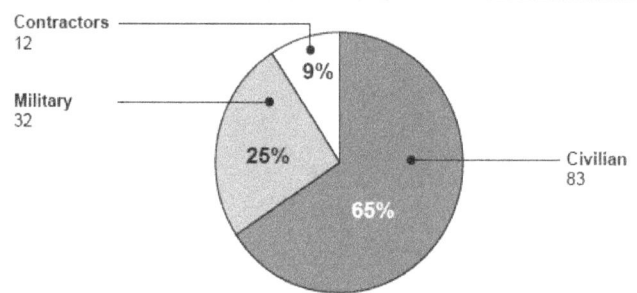

Contractors 12 — 9%

Military 32 — 25%

Civilian 83 — 65%

Total personnel: 127 (as of November 2012)

Source: GAO analysis of DOD documents.

Note: Total may not add due to rounding.

Area of Focus

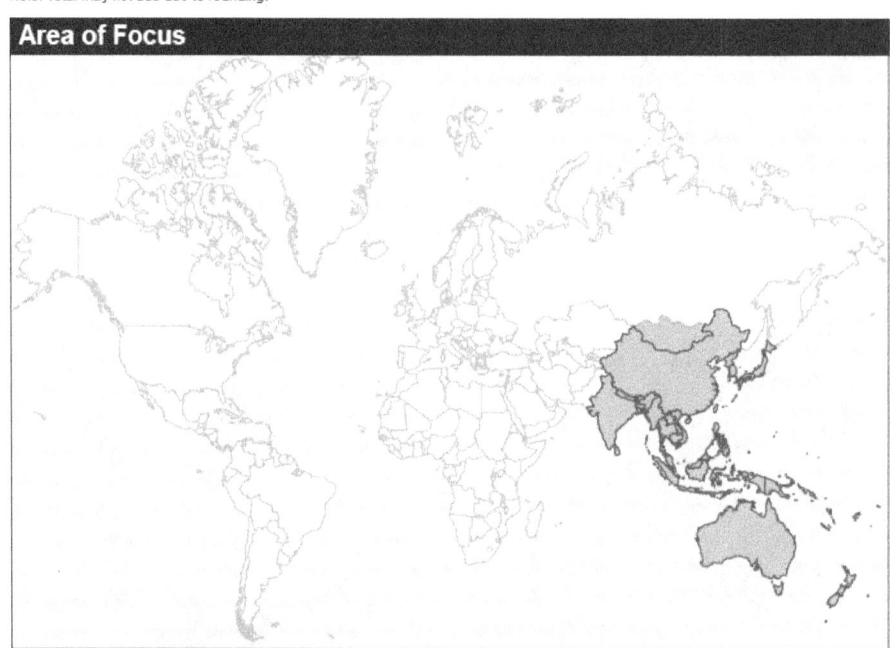

Source: GAO analysis of DOD documents.

William J. Perry Center for Hemispheric Defense Studies

About the Center

Location: Washington, D.C.

Founded: 1997

Mission: Conduct educational activities for civilians and the military in the Western Hemisphere to enhance partner capacity and foster trust, mutual understanding, and regional cooperation.

Priorities:
- Encourage whole-of-government coordination and support hemispheric coordination mechanisms to enhance information-sharing.
- Facilitate bilateral and multilateral cooperation to build common perspectives on regional challenges and greater capacity.
- Promote a strategic dialogue and communicate U.S. defense priorities to regional leaders.
- Promote partner nation defense planning and strategy development (peacekeeping, humanitarian assistance and disaster relief, stability, and counterterrorism operations).
- Support civilian military control, transitions, and oversight.

Courses:
- Governance, Governability and Security in The Americas: Responses to Transnational Organized Crime
- Nationlab
- Perspectives on Homeland Security and Homeland Defense
- Strategy and Defense Policy Course
- Washington Security and Defense Seminar

Alumni: 5,335 (as of September 2012)

Fiscal Year 2012 DOD Operation and Maintenance Funding

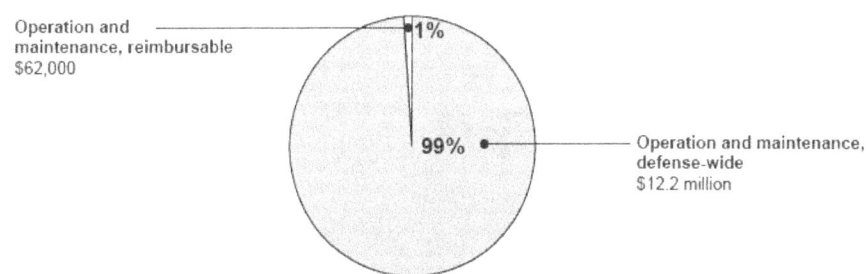

Operation and maintenance, reimbursable $62,000 — 1%

99% — Operation and maintenance, defense-wide $12.2 million

Total funding: $12.3 million

Source: GAO analysis of DOD documents.

Fiscal Year 2012 Personnel

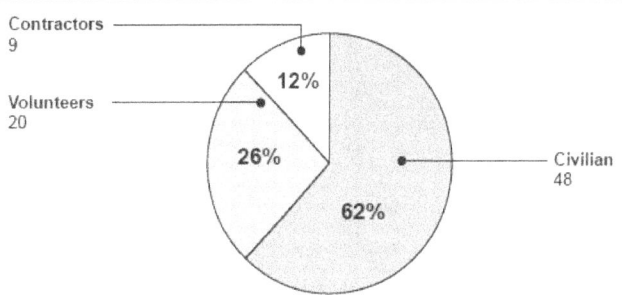

Contractors 9 — 12%

Volunteers 20 — 26%

62% — Civilian 48

Total personnel: 77 (as of September 2012)

Source: GAO analysis of DOD documents.

Area of Focus

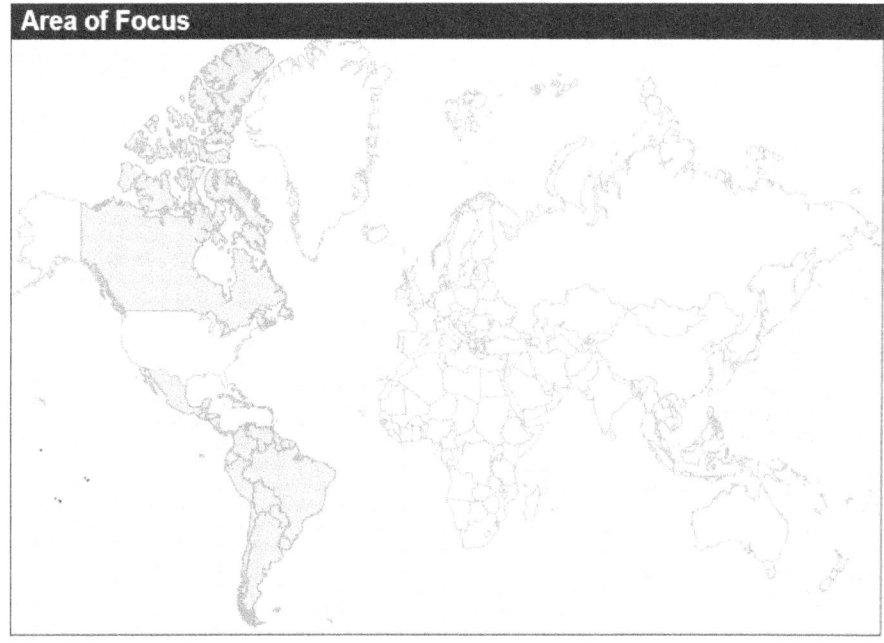

Source: GAO analysis of DOD documents.

George C. Marshall European Center for Security Studies

Source: GAO analysis of DOD documents.

About the Center

Location: Garmisch-Partenkirchen, Germany

Founded: 1993

Mission: Create a more stable security environment by advancing democratic institutions and relationships, especially in the field of defense; promoting active, peaceful security cooperation; and enhancing enduring partnerships among the nations of North America, Europe, and Eurasia.

Priorities:
- Address implications for transatlantic security organizations based on U.S. strategic rebalancing
- Emphasize engagement with U.S. European Command priority countries
- Emphasize European and Eurasian regional security issues
- Expand engagement with Central Asia on regional security, defense transformation, defense strategy development, and building partner capacity
- Sustain trans-regional counterterrorism engagement
- Transnational organized crime illicit trafficking

Courses:
- Program in Applied Security Studies—Capacity Building
- Program in Security Sector Capacity Building
- Program on Terrorism and Security Studies
- Seminar on Combating Weapons of Mass Destruction/Terrorism
- Seminar on Regional Security
- Seminar on Transatlantic Civil Security
- Senior Executive Seminar

Alumni: 9,451 (as of January 2013)

Fiscal Year 2012 DOD Operation and Maintenance Funding

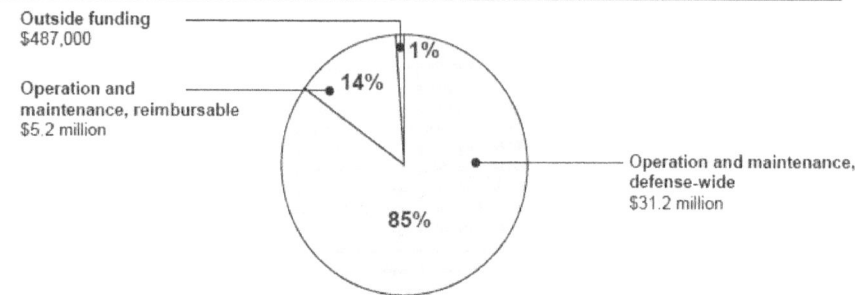

Outside funding $487,000 — 1%

Operation and maintenance, reimbursable $5.2 million — 14%

Operation and maintenance, defense-wide $31.2 million — 85%

Total funding: $36.9 million

Source: GAO analysis of DOD documents.

Fiscal Year 2012 Personnel

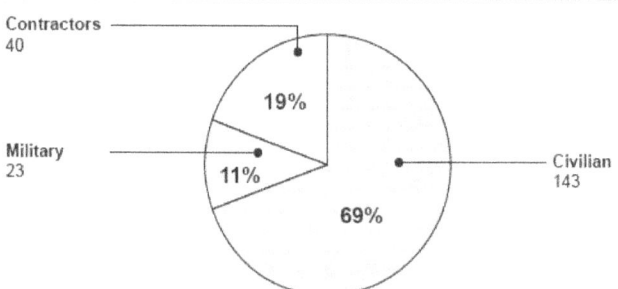

Contractors 40 — 19%

Military 23 — 11%

Civilian 143 — 69%

Total personnel: 206 (as of September 2012)

Source: GAO analysis of DOD documents.

Note: Total may not add due to rounding.

Area of Focus

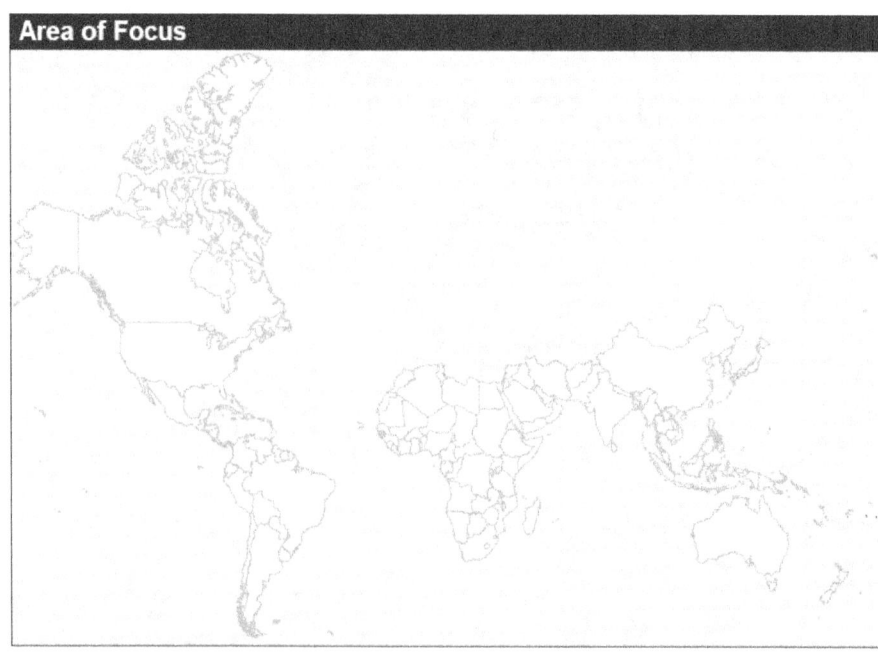

Source: GAO analysis of DOD documents.

Appendix II: The Department of Defense's (DOD) Regional Centers for Security Studies

Near East South Asia Center for Strategic Studies

Location: Washington, D.C.

Founded: 2000

Mission: To enhance stability in the Near East and South Asia region by providing a professional academic environment where the key security issues facing the region can be addressed, mutual understanding is deepened, partnerships are fostered, security related decision making is improved, and cooperation is strengthened among military and security professionals from regional countries and the United States.

Priorities:
- Focus on Afghanistan/Pakistan and Middle Eastern region security:
  - Civilian control of the military,
  - Increasing regional countering violent extremist efforts, and
  - Increasing the involvement of non-defense/Ministry of Foreign Affairs officials in programs.
- Professional military ethics
- Reform and long-term stability
- Support for international standards
- Transparency and accountability

Courses:
- U.S. Central Command Senior National Representative Seminar
- Combating Transnational Threats Executive Seminars
- Combating Transnational Threats Senior Executive Seminar
- Executive Seminars
- Senior Executive Seminar

Alumni: 3,472 (as of June 2012)

Fiscal Year 2012 DOD Operation and Maintenance Funding

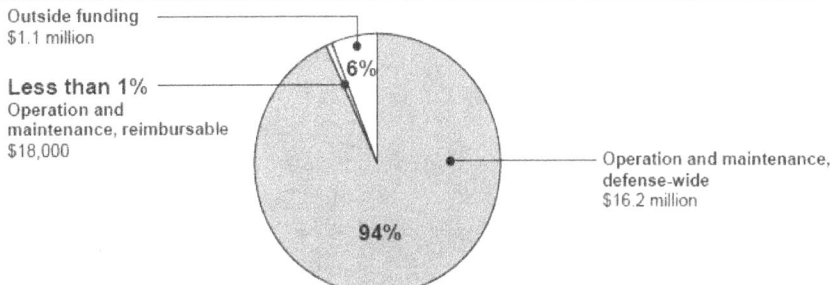

Outside funding $1.1 million — 6%

Less than 1% Operation and maintenance, reimbursable $18,000

Operation and maintenance, defense-wide $16.2 million — 94%

Total funding: $17.3 million

Source: GAO analysis of DOD documents.

Note: Total may not add due to rounding.

Fiscal Year 2012 Personnel

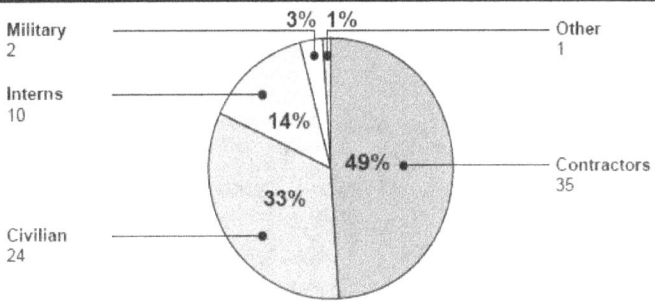

Military 2 — 3%

Interns 10 — 14%

Civilian 24 — 33%

Other 1 — 1%

Contractors 35 — 49%

Total personnel: 72 (as of September 2012)

Source: GAO analysis of DOD documents.

Area of Focus

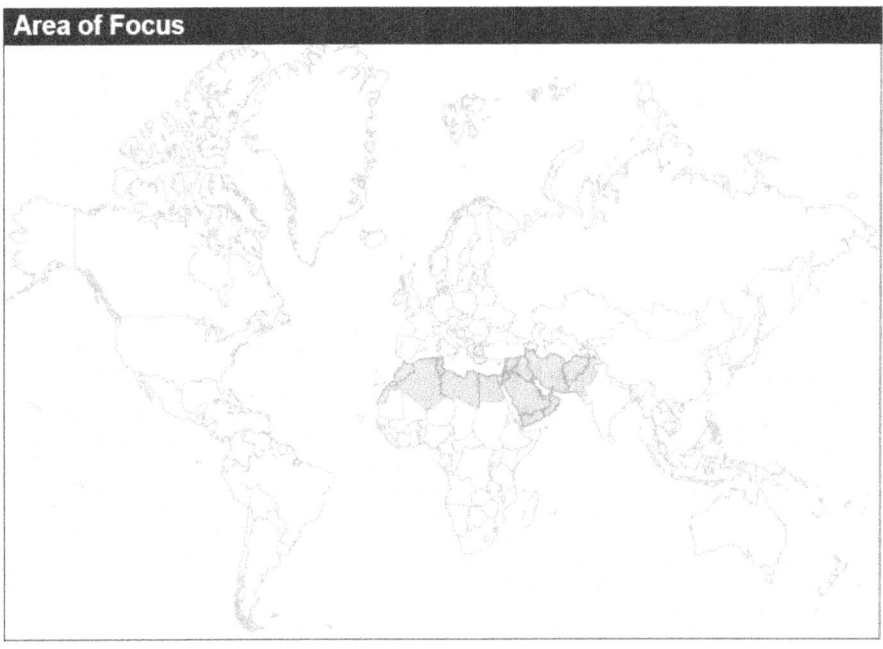

Source: GAO analysis of DOD documents.

Appendix III: Reimbursement Waivers

The Secretary of Defense may use any of several specific authorities in Title 10 U.S. Code to pay the expenses of representatives from various regions around the world to attend Department of Defense (DOD)-sponsored programs and activities, including those of the Regional Centers. These authorities vary on the basis of the type of attendees (civilian or military) as well as the region of the world from where they originate. The authority contained in 10 U.S.C. § 184note specifically applies to nongovernmental and international organization (NGO/IO) personnel attending Regional Center programs, for which DOD has issued specific guidance to govern approval of reimbursement waivers.

Multiple Authorities Exist

In fiscal year 2009, 10 U.S.C. § 184note was enacted to temporarily grant the Secretary of Defense the authority to waive reimbursement of costs for NGO/IO personnel to attend Regional Center programs.[1] Approval of waived reimbursement depends on whether the NGO/IO's attendance is deemed to be in the U.S. national security interest and is subject to the concurrence of the Secretary of State. Further, the collective reimbursements being waived may not exceed a total of $1 million (according to DOD officials, reimbursement is paid from the Regional Centers' Operation and Maintenance budgets) in any fiscal year. This temporary waiver authority has been renewed most recently through fiscal year 2013. Title 10 also contains permanent authorities to pay the expenses of foreign representatives in order to foster cooperation with various countries in those regions. Specifically, 10 U.S.C. 184(f)(3) allows the Secretary of Defense to waive reimbursement of the costs of activities of the Regional Centers for foreign military officers and foreign defense and security civilian government officials from a developing country if the Secretary determines that attendance of such personnel without reimbursement is in the national security interest of the United States. In addition, 10 U.S.C. § 1050 has been in effect since 1984 and allows the Secretary of Defense to pay the expenses of officers and students from Latin American countries.[2] In 2011, Congress enacted 10 U.S.C. § 1050a, allowing the Secretary of Defense to pay the expenses of officers and students from African countries. Under 10 U.S.C. § 113note, the

---

[1]Pub. L. No. 110-417, Div. A, Title IX, § 941(b) (Oct. 14, 2008), as amended Pub. L. No. 111-383, Div. A, Title IX, § 941 (Jan. 7, 2011); Pub. L. No. 112-239, Div. A, Title IX, § 953 (Jan. 2, 2013), (10 U.S.C. § 184note).

[2]Similar provisions had been contained in appropriations dating back to 1942.

Secretary of Defense has the ability to pay the expenses of military officers and civilian officials from European countries. The authorities are summarized in table 3.

Table 3: 10 U.S.C. Authorities

Authority	Applies to	From
10 U.S.C. § 1050	officers and students	Latin American countries
10 U.S.C. § 1050a	officers and students	African countries
10 U.S.C. § 113note	military officers and civilian officials	European countries
10 U.S.C. § 184	military officials and defense and security civilians	developing countries
10 U.S.C. § 184note	personnel	nongovernmental and international organizations (NGO/IO)

Source: GAO.

Reimbursement Waiver Approval Process under 10 U.S.C. § 184

DOD has set up specific procedures to direct the use of the authority granted under 10 U.S.C. § 184note to waive reimbursement of expenses by NGO/IOs. This procedural guidance cites national security interests when considering waiver of reimbursement and encourages the Regional Centers to request waivers on the basis of each NGO/IO's financial need. It also outlines six specific priorities to be used for determining waiver consideration, as described in table 4.

Table 4: Fiscal Year 2011 – 2013 Priorities for Waiver Consideration, in Order of Importance

Priority	Description
1	NGO/IOs that participate alongside or in the vicinity of U.S. forces during postconflict stability and/or disaster-management operations, and whose participation has a direct benefit to DOD operations.
2	NGO/IOs that participate in disaster-management and stability operations with partners.
3	NGO/IOs that play an important role in countering violent extremism.
4	NGO/IOs that provide civil society oversight of foreign partner security sectors.
5	NGO/IOs that engage in "sustainable development and stabilization" (also known as Phase Zero) activities, where U.S. or foreign partner security forces are actively engaged (e.g., health affairs).
6	NGO/IOs that broadly influence security policies in their countries or international organizations.

Source: DOD.

According to the procedural guidance issued by DOD, as well as discussions with DOD and State Department officials, the process through which waivers are requested and approved under 10 U.S.C. § 184note is as follows:

- The Regional Centers send the Defense Security Cooperation Agency (DSCA) their waiver requests identifying each organization, individual attendees, and dollar amounts, and providing justifications for their requests.
- DSCA then reviews the requests and transmits them to the Department of State's Bureau of Political-Military Affairs for its concurrence and the Office of the Under Secretary of Defense for Policy (OUSD Policy) for approval.
- The Department of State and OUSD Policy circulate the requests among their respective regional and functional bureaus, which perform a review of each candidate organization, principally to ensure that the organization's participation would not undermine the program's purpose.
- The Department of State transmits its concurrence to DSCA which, in turn, notifies OUSD Policy of the concurrence. OUSD Policy transmits its approvals to DSCA.
- DSCA designates a portion of the $1 million total waiver authority to each Regional Center, setting a cap on how much of each center's Operation and Maintenance budget may be spent on waiving reimbursements by NGO/IOs attending their programs.

Use of Other Authorities

In addition to the legislative authority provided for waiver of reimbursement for NGO/IO personnel, OUSD Policy and the Regional Centers may use other Title 10 authorities granted to the Secretary of Defense. To date, only the William J. Perry Center for Hemispheric Defense Studies has paid the expenses of NGO/IO personnel with an authority other than 10 U.S.C. § 184note. Using the authority under 10 U.S.C. § 1050, whereby the Secretary of Defense may pay the expenses of officers and students from Latin American countries, the William J. Perry Center for Hemispheric Defense Studies has paid the expenses of NGO/IO personnel. According to DOD, the Regional Centers have not used 10 U.S.C. § 1050a, whereby the Secretary of Defense may pay the expenses of officers and students from African countries; or 10 U.S.C. § 113note, through which the Secretary of Defense has the ability to pay the expenses of military officers and civilian officials from European countries, to waive reimbursements for participating NGO/IOs. Table 5 shows the extent to which the Regional Centers have used Title 10 authorities each fiscal year since 2009 to cover expenses for NGO/IO personnel attending their programs.

Table 5: Use of Authorities by Regional Centers to Waive NGO/IO Reimbursements, Fiscal Years 2009 through 2012

Current year dollars

	Fiscal year			
Authority/Regional Center	**2009**	**2010**	**2011**	**2012**
10 U.S.C. § 184note				
Africa Center for Strategic Studies	0	33,785	50,900	0
Asia-Pacific Center for Security Studies	15,797	13,794	0	67,035
George C. Marshall European Center for Security Studies	0	56,000	10,500	4,648
Near East South Asia Center for Strategic Studies	78,586	33,900	133,300	0
10 U.S.C. § 184note total	**$94,383**	**$137,479**	**$194,700**	**$71,683**
10 U.S.C. § 1050				
William J. Perry Center for Hemispheric Defense Studies	573,110	579,800	251,750	333,363
Grand total	**$667,493**	**$717,279**	**$446,450**	**$405,046**

Source: GAO analysis of DOD data.

Appendix IV: Comments from the Department of Defense

UNDER SECRETARY OF DEFENSE
2000 DEFENSE PENTAGON
WASHINGTON, D.C. 20301-2000

POLICY

JUN 17 2013

Ms. Sharon Pickup
Director, Defense Capabilities and Management
U.S. Government Accountability Office
441 G Street, N.W.
Washington, DC 20548

Dear Ms. Pickup:

Enclosed is the Department of Defense (DoD) response to the May 22. 2013, GAO Draft

Report, GAO-13-606, "BUILDING PARTNER CAPACITY: Actions Needed to Strengthen

DoD Efforts to Assess the Performance of the Regional Centers for Security Studies," (GAO

Code 351753). Detailed comments on the report recommendations are also enclosed.

Sincerely,

James N. Miller

Enclosure:
As stated

GAO DRAFT REPORT DATED MAY 22, 2013
GAO-13-606 (GAO CODE 351753)

"BUILDING PARTNER CAPACITY: Actions Needed to Strengthen DoD Efforts to Assess
the Performance of the Regional Centers for Security Studies"

DEPARTMENT OF DEFENSE COMMENTS
TO THE GAO RECOMMENDATION

To enhance DoD's ability to determine whether the Regional Centers are achieving departmental
priorities, GAO recommends that the Secretary of Defense direct the Office of the Under
Secretary of Policy to:

RECOMMENDATION 1: Develop an approach to assess the Regional Centers' progress in
achieving DoD priorities, including identifying measurable goals and objectives, metrics, or
other indicators of performance.

DoD RESPONSE: Partially concur. The present recommendation should take into account that
a process already exists for Regional Center program development and approval, which requires
the Regional Centers to identify specific program goals that meet policy objectives. The
Department recognized the need to improve the identification of measurable goals and
objectives, metrics, or other indicators of performance and is already taking steps to address this
issue.

Recommend the GAO revise its recommendation as follows: "Bolster the current approach to
assess the Regional Centers' progress in achieving DOD priorities, including identifying
measurable goals and objectives, metrics, or other indicators of performance that appropriately
measure the essential aspects of the Regional Centers' mission."

RECOMMENDATION 2: Develop a methodology for using performance information, to
include defining the role of the governance board in the process.

DoD RESPONSE: Concur.

Appendix V: GAO Contacts and Staff Acknowledgments

GAO Contacts	Sharon L. Pickup, (202) 512-9619 or pickups@gao.gov
	Charles Michael Johnson, Jr., (202) 512-7331 or johnsoncm@gao.gov
Staff Acknowledgments	In addition to the contacts named above, Matthew Ullengren, Assistant Director; Judith McCloskey, Assistant Director; David Keefer; Ricardo Marquez; Shirley Min; Jamilah Moon; Amie Steele; Michael Silver; Sabrina Streagle; and Cheryl Weissman made key contributions to this report.

Related GAO Products

U.S. Assistance to Yemen: Actions Needed to Improve Oversight of Emergency Food Aid and Assess Security Assistance. GAO-13-310. Washington, D.C.: March 20, 2013

Security Assistance: Evaluations Needed to Determine Effectiveness of U.S. Aid to Lebanon's Security Forces. GAO-13-289. Washington, D.C.: March 19, 2013

Building Partner Capacity: Key Practices to Effectively Manage Department of Defense Efforts to Promote Security Cooperation. GAO-13-335T. Washington, D.C.: February 14, 2013.

Security Assistance: DOD's Ongoing Reforms Address Some Challenges, but Additional Information Is Needed to Further Enhance Program Management. GAO-13-84. Washington, D.C.: November 16, 2012.

State Partnership Program: Improved Oversight, Guidance, and Training Needed for National Guard's Efforts with Foreign Partners. GAO-12-548. Washington, D.C.: May 15, 2012.

Security Force Assistance: Additional Actions Needed to Guide Geographic Combatant Command and Service Efforts. GAO-12-556. Washington, D.C.: May 10, 2012.

Humanitarian and Development Assistance: Project Evaluations and Better Information Sharing Needed to Manage the Military's Efforts. GAO-12-359. Washington, D.C.: February 8, 2012.

Performance Measurement and Evaluation: Definitions and Relationships. GAO-11-646SP. Washington, D.C.: May 2, 2011.

Preventing Sexual Harassment: DOD Needs Greater Leadership Commitment and an Oversight Framework. GAO-11-809. Washington, D.C.: September 21, 2011.

Defense Management: U.S. Southern Command Demonstrates Interagency Collaboration, but Its Haiti Disaster Response Revealed Challenges Conducting a Large Military Operation. GAO-10-801. Washington, D.C.: July 28, 2010.

Defense Management: Improved Planning, Training, and Interagency Collaboration Could Strengthen DOD's Efforts in Africa. GAO-10-794. Washington, D.C.: July 28, 2010.

Drug Control: DOD Needs to Improve Its Performance Measurement System to Better Manage and Oversee Its Counternarcotics Activities. GAO-10-835. Washington, D.C.: July 21, 2010.

Defense Management: DOD Needs to Determine the Future of Its Horn of Africa Task Force. GAO-10-504. Washington, D.C.: April 15, 2010.

GAO's Mission	The Government Accountability Office, the audit, evaluation, and investigative arm of Congress, exists to support Congress in meeting its constitutional responsibilities and to help improve the performance and accountability of the federal government for the American people. GAO examines the use of public funds; evaluates federal programs and policies; and provides analyses, recommendations, and other assistance to help Congress make informed oversight, policy, and funding decisions. GAO's commitment to good government is reflected in its core values of accountability, integrity, and reliability.
Obtaining Copies of GAO Reports and Testimony	The fastest and easiest way to obtain copies of GAO documents at no cost is through GAO's website (http://www.gao.gov). Each weekday afternoon, GAO posts on its website newly released reports, testimony, and correspondence. To have GAO e-mail you a list of newly posted products, go to http://www.gao.gov and select "E-mail Updates."
Order by Phone	The price of each GAO publication reflects GAO's actual cost of production and distribution and depends on the number of pages in the publication and whether the publication is printed in color or black and white. Pricing and ordering information is posted on GAO's website, http://www.gao.gov/ordering.htm.
	Place orders by calling (202) 512-6000, toll free (866) 801-7077, or TDD (202) 512-2537.
	Orders may be paid for using American Express, Discover Card, MasterCard, Visa, check, or money order. Call for additional information.
Connect with GAO	Connect with GAO on Facebook, Flickr, Twitter, and YouTube. Subscribe to our RSS Feeds or E-mail Updates. Listen to our Podcasts. Visit GAO on the web at www.gao.gov.
To Report Fraud, Waste, and Abuse in Federal Programs	Contact:
	Website: http://www.gao.gov/fraudnet/fraudnet.htm E-mail: fraudnet@gao.gov Automated answering system: (800) 424-5454 or (202) 512-7470
Congressional Relations	Katherine Siggerud, Managing Director, siggerudk@gao.gov, (202) 512-4400, U.S. Government Accountability Office, 441 G Street NW, Room 7125, Washington, DC 20548
Public Affairs	Chuck Young, Managing Director, youngc1@gao.gov, (202) 512-4800 U.S. Government Accountability Office, 441 G Street NW, Room 7149 Washington, DC 20548

Please Print on Recycled Paper.